My First Words
A - Z
English to French

Bilingual Learning Made Fun and Easy with Words and Pictures

by Sharon Purtill

Books

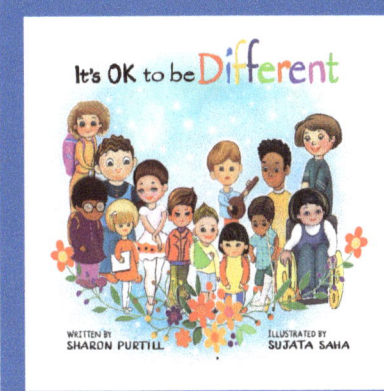

Livres

Mes premiers mots
de l'anglais vers le français

My First Words A-Z
English to French

Bilingual Learning Made Fun and Easy with Words and Pictures

by Sharon Purtill

Published by Dunhill Clare Publishing - Ontario, Canada
Copyright 2021 Dunhill Clare Publishing
dunhillclare@gmail.

Edited by Malak Ben Abdallah

All rights reserved. No part of this publication may be reproduced, stored in a retrieval system or transmitted, in any form or by any means, electronic, mechanical, photocopying, recording or otherwise without the prior permission of the copyright holder except when embodied in a brief review or mention.

Paperback edition ISBN: 978-1-989733-76-9
Digital edition   ISBN: 978-1-989733-77-6

Library and Archives Canada Cataloguing in Publications

Apple

Pomme

Books

Livres

Cat

Chat

Dog

Chien

Elephant

Éléphant

Flower

Fleur

Giraffe

Girafe

Hat

Chapeau

Ice Cream

Crème glacée

Jacket

Veste

Keys

Clés

Leaf

Feuille

Milk

Lait

Nest

Nid

Orange

Orange

Pail

Seau

Quilt

Couette

Rabbit

Lapin

Shoe

Chaussure

Table

Table

Umbrella

Parapluie

Vacuum

Aspirateur

Watermelon

Pastèque

Xylophone

Xylophone

Yellow

Jaune

Zebra

Zèbre

Bonus Words

English and French

Let's learn common words for things found in and around the home.

oh what FUN

Found in the Kitchen
Trouvé dans la cuisine

plate		assiette
fork		fourchette
spoon		cuillère
knife		couteau
bowl		bol
cup		tasse

Found in the Bathroom
Trouvé dans la salle de bain

toothpaste  dentifrice

toothbrush  brosse à dents

brush  brosse

comb  peigne

towel  serviette

Found in the Bedroom
Trouvé dans la chambre

bed  lit

blankets  couvertures

pillow  oreiller

dresser  commode

toys  jouets

Found in the Living Room
Trouvé dans le salon

television		télévision
armchair		fauteuil
rug		tapis
lamp		lampe
sofa		canapé

Found Outside
Trouvé à l'extérieur

tree  arbre

car  voiture

truck  camion

bike  bicyclette

grass  gazon

www.ingramcontent.com/pod-product-compliance
Lightning Source LLC
Chambersburg PA
CBHW050740080526
44579CB00017B/110